Contents

Dedicated to:

My mom and dad,
my husband, Curtis,
and my children, Dana, Anthony,
and Treasure.

Introduction:

Balance Defined

What is balance, and what does it look like in life? I would define achieving balance as living life to the fullest, with each facet of your life enjoying the right amount of attention and functioning at its fullest potential. True balance in life is the secret to personal happiness, marital success, happy and well-adjusted children, and a flourishing career. When we are truly balanced, we enjoy a state of contentment. Even when bad experiences come our way, we are able to ride the storm with a sense of peace that would amaze those looking on.

The opposite of balance may be easier to define, as we feel this way much of the time. When we're unbalanced, we feel like we have lost control, and life feels like it's falling apart. When we're unbalanced, we may appear to be doing well in certain areas (e.g., our work), while other areas are falling apart (e.g., relationships at home). You may lead a successful career, but your children barely know you, and you barely know them. Perhaps you work yourself to the bones as lack of sleep and proper nutrition lead to poor health and disability. Or maybe you have the perfect family and career, yet inside you feel empty, lonely, or depressed. Imbalance often threatens to define us. It can lead to marital discord, broken homes, poor work performance, poor mental and physical health, and, ultimately, unhappiness.

The search for true balance in life motivated me to write this book. The title, *Achieving Balance*, is deliberate, as one never truly arrives. Once attained, it can be lost. Rather, we have to constantly adapt and adjust areas of our life to maintain a healthy balance. Every day, there will be challenges to our sense of balance, that sense of inner peace and contentment. Think of your life as a hurdling race. With each stride, there is another hurdle. Your goal is to keep running and, even if you fall, to get up and keep going. There are many factors that affect our sense of balance, such that achieving and maintaining balance becomes a daily if not hourly struggle.

While the need for balance in life is not unique to women, the life of a working mother is a prime example of imbalance. A working wife and mother wears several hats and is frequently pulled in multiple directions at once. She has to attend to the needs of her husband, care for her children, and still fulfill the demands of her career. When it all works well, everyone is happy and she is the embodiment of Proverbs 31's description of a virtuous woman. But when the balance of her duties is not maintained, things fall apart, making everyone involved unhappy.

Let me share with you a day in my life that exemplifies the working mother's typical struggle. It's Monday morning, and I get up a little late and tired from the weekend. I struggle to get myself together, but my hair is not cooperating. I run out of time to make it better because I have to get my two kids ready for daycare and school. They are three and seven years old. We are running behind as I get them into the car. My three-year-old has decided it's time to go potty. Unlucky for me, she's at a daycare that does not allow you to bring your child in with a dirty diaper. The thoughtful daycare lady makes me change her before I can leave.

By then, I have just five minutes left to get the seven-year-old to school on time. He gets to school late, and I feel so much mommy guilt knowing he is late because of me. I eventually make it to work, and I have to put my

bad hair day and horrible morning experience aside to attend to patient after patient,
being sure to attend to their needs and not
let my "stuff" distract me or get in the way.
So, I do my best. I pace myself and make it
through without killing anyone or making any
negligent medical mistakes, only to get home
completely exhausted with little to give to my
husband and two young children. This is an
example of the lack of balance.

When we lack balance, we feel over-
whelmed. We feel like we've lost control and
things are falling apart. This imbalance, if
unchecked, can lead to stress, depression,
and unhappiness for everyone involved.

Fast-forward to a couple of years later. It's
a crisp fall morning in Buckhead, Atlanta. It's
Sunday, and I'm sitting in my SUV with my kids
in the backseat. My now nine-year-old son is
avidly reading his new Minecraft book that he
just got from Barnes & Noble. I'm parked just
outside the store, not in a rush to go anywhere.

My five-year-old is coloring in her new coloring book. I am poised to start reading a novel I just purchased. I have not read a novel to completion in years because I never had the time. We are waiting for my husband, who is in a business meeting concerning a counseling business he has recently purchased.

I'm feeling great, more content and at peace than I have felt in a long time. I'm feeling blessed. My marriage is going well. My kids are thriving and doing well at school. They have adjusted well to our new home. (We moved a few months prior.)

When my husband is done with his meeting, we plan to have lunch together at one of our favorite restaurants in the area and then surprise the kids by taking them to a Disney musical. I'm looking forward to seeing their reactions when we pull up to the theater!

So, this is what balance feels like. We both still work, but here we are, enjoying quality family time with those who mean the most to us while still enjoying flourishing careers, good health, and marital happiness. How did we get here in just two years? Read on as I share some secrets to achieving balance in a hectic and demanding world.

Chapter 1

Choosing to Pursue
Your Career

Proverbs 31:17–18
"She girds herself with strength,
And strengthens her arms.
She perceives that her
merchandise is good,
And her lamp does not go out by night."

T oday, the number of women in colleges in the United States outnumber the number of men, and this has been the case for many years. This may be due in part to the feminist movement, which fought for equal treatment of women and men under the law, voting rights for women, equal pay for men and women doing the same job, and equal rights for women in many other areas of life, especially education. As the women's liberation movement evolved, colleges saw higher enrollment of women. As a result, more women entered the workforce and became gainfully employed outside of the home.

I grew up in the 1970s and 1980s. I was encouraged to pursue college education. Many people, including me, thought I should not stop my academic pursuits with a high school diploma. So, I pursued college, got in, and did extremely well. I then applied to and got into medical school, where just over 50 percent of my classmates and the graduating class were female.

So, why is this important? Well, the pursuit of higher education was unchartered territory for women in my generation. You see, my grandmother's generation had worked mainly in the home. They did the cooking, housecleaning, child–rearing, and laundering. If they worked outside of the house, it was mainly to clean someone else's home or office. This would give them a little cash for their personal needs or wishes. They depended almost entirely on their husbands for financial support and security. My mother's generation, women of the 1950s and 60s, ventured a little further. My mother completed high school and got an office job as a clerk. She later pursued studies in nursing and enjoyed this change in her career. My father attended teacher's training college in Trinidad and became a high school art teacher. So, during my childhood, I was raised by two parents who worked outside the home. We did not live far from my grandmother, who cared for us when my mother could not be there. My grandmother or my aunt would watch my cousins, my siblings, and me while my mother and father worked.

The thought of a woman staying home and doing mainly housework and childcare was never my vision for life. I spent a lot of time reading when I was a child. Some of my earliest memories involve me reading health encyclopedias that my parents kept on a bookshelf at home. I would go on to do well in elementary school. My academic success began when I passed my high school entrance exam for one of the best high schools in my home country of Tobago. I attended Bishop's High School in Tobago and did well in my final exams, with grades equivalent to the American 4.0 grade point average.

Indeed, I was quite the nerd. My academic success was well publicized in my home country, so much so that others took great interest in what I would do after high school. For many children in Tobago, a high school diploma was considered the completion of one's education. Many got jobs in the public service, the banks, the schools, or in government agencies.

Upon leaving high school, I worked for a few months at the public library, but it was not long before I departed the shores of my home country to pursue college education in the United States. In this, too, I was a pioneer. Not only was I the first member of my family to pursue a college education, but I was one of few at that time who left our small Caribbean island to pursue studies in the United States. This was an awesome opportunity, and I had to make the best of it.

Being able to choose to go to college and pursue a career was a blessing. It was also exciting! I was embarking on unchartered territory for women in my country. I had few role models who were women. I recall reading the books *Think Big* and *Gifted Hands* by Dr. Ben Carson. They inspired me to dream big and toy with the idea of becoming a doctor. But that thought would not take serious shape until I was well into my college years.

I was grateful to have the opportunity to pursue higher education, and I endeavored even more to excel. I promised God that I would make straight A's in my first semester in college as a "thank you" for Him giving me a full scholarship. Not only did I get straight A's in my first semester, but every semester after that. I graduated from Morgan State University in Baltimore, Maryland, summa cum laude with a 4.0 grade point average. I would later pursue the study of medicine in Southern California.

There was never another option for me but to pursue my career. I was excited, and I loved every minute of school. I loved reading and learning. Medical school was like the icing on the cake for me. My parents were so proud of me; I was the first doctor in the family.

As a physician, I later gave a talk at a church function on health. After my talk, a young lady came up to me. She had to have been about fifteen or sixteen years old. She wanted to know how I balanced being a physician, a wife, and a mother. She was interested in going to college after completing high school, but she feared that she would have difficulty finding a husband and being a good mother as well. I encouraged her to pursue her dreams and to not abandon her educational goals, because there is nothing better than to pursue one's vision or purpose for one's life.

The question from that young lady stuck with me for years, and it has inspired me to share my journey with others. Who knows how many other young women are holding back on their academic dreams for fear of intimating others, or being unable to balance their work and family life. The delicate dance of balancing career and family is what this book is about. I seek to share what I have learned along the way with those who wish to know how I do my balancing act.

Some women fear that pursing their career will make them overqualified or intimidating to men. To those women, I say that the man who is intimidated by your success is likely not the man for you. Some men need to feel powerful by exercising dominion and control over women. If you choose to limit yourself and your potential to please such men, that is your choice. But know that there are accomplished and confident men who are not intimidated or threatened by intelligent, successful women. Barack and Michelle Obama are a prime example of a couple who supports one another's careers without limiting the woman's education or academic pursuits in order for the man to feel more powerful.

Women today should pursue the career of their dreams. The question is how to balance her roles if she chooses to also get married and have kids. Several factors will affect her ability to balance these roles. Much depends on the man she marries and whether he also has a busy career, or if he can stay home and help with childcare as his wife pursues her career. As a woman in medicine, I have met several colleagues for whom this option works well. Alternatively, she may choose to pursue her career part-time rather than full-time, which affords her more time to perform her duties as wife and mother. There are also women who take a hiatus from their careers for a few years as they raise their young children. These are all viable options for working mothers. The option you chose should be one that works for you. Some will argue that one choice is better than another, but what works for one woman may not work for another, so chose the option that works for you and your family.

The path you chose will definitely have consequences. If you chose to stay at home or even work part-time, you will likely not have benefits like health insurance and retirement savings, although you may be able to get insurance through your spouse. Women in this position are dependent on their husbands to provide these important benefits for them and their children. What happens then if, God forbid, the husband dies or the marriage ends? The woman will then find herself unemployed and dependent on others to support herself and her children. Unless their husband or significant other has made special provisions, these women risk an insecure future unless they reenter the workforce later on.

For women who aspire to pursue their careers and be financially independent, it is wise to seek out role models in the field they wish to pursue. In today's world, there is no shortage of successful women in just about every field imaginable. There are female doctors, lawyers, engineers, astronauts, teachers, principals, judges, pastors, professors, governors, mayors, and congresswomen. We nearly had our first female president in the person of Hillary Clinton. She has paved the way for other women to aspire to this great office. Because of women like her and many others, young girls today are growing up with the hope of being whatever they wish to be. This is indeed an awesome thing.

By choosing to pursue your career, you are choosing to live life to its fullest potential, to pursue your God-given purpose, and to be of useful service to your community. You will achieve economic stability and security for your future and for the futures of your children. Pursuing your academic and career goals does not make you any less of a woman, wife, or mother. I hope this book will help you see that it is possible to achieve work-life balance without sacrificing your career.

Chapter 2

Marriage: The Primary Relationship

Genesis 2:24

"Therefore a man shall leave his father and mother and be joined to his wife, and they shall become one flesh."

L et's say you've met the person you want to share your life with. You are super excited! Soon you will plan a glorious wedding, inviting your dearest friends and family members to celebrate with you as you start a new chapter in life. Dating was not much of a problem. You got dressed up and went out to fine restaurants and the movies. You even took a few trips together to meet each other's families. Now as you walk down the aisle, say your "I dos," and bid your friends and family members adieu, you are launched into a new world that you have little preparation for and no test trial. You return from the honeymoon and settle into this new world with little guidance on how to navigate the realities of being married.

Before being married, you spent a few hours with your beloved, all dressed up and looking your best. Now you're with your beloved day in and day out, ready or not, as you truly are. He gets to see you at your best and worst. Being married is not "happily ever after." Instead, it's sharing life with all its ups and downs, unexpected surprises, and day-to-day challenges. But achieving balance even during the various challenges of life can help a marriage thrive and be successful.

As you enter marriage, real-life struggles begin to affect your new world. After all, in order to maintain your lifestyle, someone has to pay the bills. One or both of you have to go to work. It's not like the honeymoon, where you drink piña coladas and eat hors d'oeuvres twenty-four-seven on a beautiful island. Now someone has to cook so you don't starve to death. And while eating out may have been an enjoyable part of dating, it certainly cannot be your source of every meal once you're married unless you plan to go bankrupt.

You also have to maintain some cleanliness and order in your home, whether it's a tiny apartment or your first house. You will soon discover how easily it gets messed up and covered in dust, and how much time it takes to get the dust off and put things back in order. Your day-to-day clothing has to be washed and ironed, or dry-cleaned if necessary. Someone has to do this or you will both soon run out of underwear! Then, if you choose to have children, you will be doing all of this not only for the two of you, but also for your fully dependent newborn, toddler, and eventually pre-schooler as well.

It's easy to see how the activities of daily living and survival can soon occupy your every ounce of energy during every waking moment, so much so that you can lose sight of your primary relationship: the marriage. While I am not a relationship expert (although my husband can claim this title), making your marriage the primary priority must be a deliberate choice for both of you. It doesn't just happen, especially after the birth of your children. You need to make time for your spouse amid the busyness of life's demands.

As a couple, decide how the housework will be handled. If you are a two-income family, it may be difficult for you to handle all of the housework as well. You may choose to share the load between the two of you, or you may decide it's best to hire a housekeeper. Some couples may decide to hire a live-in housekeeper to keep the house clean at all times, while others may choose to have someone come weekly or biweekly to do general cleaning. Either way, you need to decide what works for your household and budget. Whatever you decide, work to maintain the cleanliness and happiness in your home.

With regard to children, it is important to set boundaries from an early age. Co-sleeping with your child is not a good idea unless you're ready to end your marriage. Having a child sleep in a bassinet in your room during the first few weeks after their birth is totally understandable, but getting your children to sleep in their own crib at an early age is important for the marriage relationship and for the child.

Finding dependable childcare is also essential to maintaining a happy marriage. If you are blessed to have your mother, mother-in-law, or a dependable family member available, be grateful for their assistance, as many do not enjoy such a luxury. If you don't have a family member available, you will need to undertake the difficult task of hiring a nanny or babysitter, or finding a reputable daycare center to help with your childcare needs. You can try to go it alone, but getting help with childcare is important for your health and sanity.

Nurturing your primary relationship means prioritizing your marriage despite the demands of your busy life. A short phone call in the middle of the workday does wonders. Better yet, showing up and taking your spouse out for lunch or dropping off lunch for your spouse in the middle of the day goes a long way to keep your spouse's attention during the course of a busy day. It's nice to have a date night for just the two of you. These moments give you the opportunity to reconnect with your spouse in ways you can't do when you're at home dealing with the demands of work, childcare, and household chores.

Make time for the two of you to connect intellectually, physically, and spiritually. This requires spending quality time together, which can be difficult if you both have demanding schedules. But there are a few simple things you can do to connect with your spouse on a meaningful level. Here are four steps you can

take to maintain marital romance and connectivity despite the demands of life.

Step 1: Sleep together.

Step one may sound like a no-brainer.
You may say to yourself, "Don't all couples
sleep together?" The answer to this question
may surprise you. There are many reasons
couples get into different sleeping routines
and habits.

Some people consider themselves to be
night owls, meaning they are most productive during the late hours of the night. Others
consider themselves to be morning people;
they get up early and accomplish many tasks
in the early-morning hours. They may feel
refreshed after several hours of sleep, and
therefore have the mental clarity and physical strength to get many things done early in
the day. If a husband and wife are on different
ends of this spectrum, they can end up going

to bed and waking up at very different times. The wife may go to bed at 10 p.m. and get up at 4 or 5 a.m., while the husband, who is a night owl, can stay up until 1 a.m. and sleep until 6 or 7 a.m. Knowing that his wife wakes up around 5 a.m., the husband may opt to sleep in a different room so as to not be disturbed in the early morning hours.

For other couples, their sleeping arrangements may be dictated by a difference in work schedules. If one spouse works at night several times a week and the other works in the day, their sleeping habits are going to be different. For other couples, issues of ill health affect sleeping habits. A person with sleep apnea or congestive heart failure may need to sleep with a CPAP machine or sitting up in a recliner. This can impact the other partner and lead them to sleep in separate areas. And then, of course, there is the periodic argument that can lead to one party sleeping on the couch for the night. These are all scenarios that can prevent couples from sleeping together, which leads to discord and poor connectivity between spouses.

Sleeping together is important for keeping spouses connected and in tune with each other. Going to bed at the same time allows couples to share in the routine of preparing for sleep, allows time for cuddling, pillow talk and ultimately sexual intimacy. The psychological and physical connection that occurs when going to bed together can be more difficult to achieve if spouses are sleeping apart.

For couples who work different hours or go to bed at different times for reasons of ill health or work schedules, it's important to find other times for this level of intimacy, perhaps on weekends, or as much as possible during the week. For couples with health issues, sexual intimacy may not be a priority, but it would still be important to spend quality time together communicating each other's feelings and needs.

Step 2: Eat together.

Another way to stay connected with one's spouse is to enjoy one or more meals together each day. The demands of work or school for the kids may have everyone grabbing the quickest meal they can on the go. However, couples and families should make deliberate efforts to have meals together at a specified time. At dinnertime, they can debrief with each other about the happenings of the day, or simply enjoy each other's company at the end of a long day. Sharing a meal together is one of the most effective bonding rituals spouses and families can practice.

Of course, the occasional date night when the couple enjoys dinner at a restaurant or takes food out to dine at home is also a smart way of dining together without having to prepare or clean up after the meal. Indeed, happy couples can maintain marital harmony and connectivity simply by sharing a meal.

Step 3: Play together.

How can couples play together? This essentially means engaging in activities that you both enjoy. It may be going to a movie, play, or comedy show. It may even be an impromptu weekend trip or getaway. It may be a night out on the town with some friends. Whatever you enjoy doing should be done together as much as possible. It's important that couples who work hard also find time to play hard and have fun with each other.

Playing together can also mean sharing simply pleasures together, such as going for a morning walk or an evening stroll in the park. It could also be sharing a picnic in the park with the kids, or an evening at the beach watching the sunset. Again, it does not have to be anything expensive or elaborate. Marriage is about sharing life together, and finding ways to enjoy the simple pleasures in life is a great way to make playful and fun memories.

Step 4: Pray together.

This step has to do with sharing a spiritual connection. It has been shown that couples that pray together stay together. Attending some kind of religious service together and enjoying spiritually uplifting moments can do wonders to help couples stay connected, especially when dealing with various dilemmas. This strengthens the marital bond and gives hope especially during times of weakness. It can also bring healing and restoration after discord and disagreement.

In essence, to maintain marital harmony and withstand the trials of day-to-day stressors, it's the simple acts of life like sleeping, eating, playing, and praying together that couples need on a regular basis.

Many couples may argue that it's not that simple to maintain marital bliss and harmony. Even while doing all the things mentioned above, couples may still struggle to maintain a true connection with each other. With the demands of your careers and the care of the kids, it is easy to put your marriage on the back burner and let it fend for itself. However, you have to choose to be and stay married, no matter what. You must choose to not let your primary relationship suffer under the other demands of life. Your marriage is like a plant: it needs to be watered and groomed to achieve the best growth and resilience. To prioritize your marriage, you need to nurture and guard it fiercely.

It is healthy for couples to seek out counseling even when their marriage is doing well. The same person who did your premarital counseling may be an ideal person to go back to in six months, one year, or five years after the wedding. Going back for regular checkups will help you analyze how things are going. It's OK to seek out a new counselor as well who can help with issues in your marriage. In any case, find a counselor who can evaluate the areas that are working well in your marriage while also determining what areas need improvement, along with steps to get there.

When we take the four steps listed above, we deliberately strengthen our union, not allowing our relationships to be battered by the winds. Couples must take bold steps to declare to the world that they are truly one. Outward displays of affection can help strengthen your union and display your unity to others. It's important to sit together at church or other social gatherings, to go for walks and hold hands as if you are still dating, to wear matching outfits, and to drive together in the same car.

It's amazing how many married couples live in the same house but lead separate lives. Resist the temptation to live singly while married. Put the work in to keep your marriage blissful and happy; you will be happier for it, and so will your family and the community around you.

Chapter 3:

Baby Makes Three. Now What?

Psalm 127:3
"Behold, children are a
heritage from the LORD,
The fruit of the womb is a reward."

C ongratulations are in order; you have a new addition to the family. Welcome to your new normal. Before baby, it was just the two of you. You still had a reasonable amount of personal and couple time. But when baby arrives, the dynamics of your relationship change almost overnight. You now have to deal with little or no sleep. Much of your attention has to be placed on this new life that is fully dependent on you for its care and survival. Your focus and attention is now divided between work, marriage, and parenthood.

So, how do you maintain balance in your life after your children arrive? How do you find time to spend together as a couple after the babies? And what about time for yourself? Is it possible to maintain a healthy balance after you become a parent? That is the focus of this chapter.

When a new baby arrives, there is much excitement. In many cases, family members come to meet the new addition and to help in any way they can. In time, they return to their own lives, leaving you to yours. This is when you need to figure a few things out.

As a new parent, you have many decisions to make. Will you return to work at the same capacity you did before? Can you return to work part-time? Or will you stay home with baby for a number of years? Do you have someone to help with childcare? For the new mom, one option is to have her mother or mother-in-law help out. But for many, grand-parents may not be accessible. Due to issues like ailing health or geographic distance, many don't have family members who can lend a hand in childcare.

If you choose to be a stay-at-home mom, you may be tempted to think that maintaining balance does not apply to you. However, it may apply to you even more because it's even more difficult to set boundaries between work time, family time, and personal time. If you are always present to attend to your child's every need, you may neglect your marital and self-care needs at times. You still need to eat healthy meals, exercise, and get adequate rest. You still need to spend quality time with your spouse, friends, and other adults. Even for the stay-at-home mom, childcare assistance may be needed at times to help you take care of yourself.

Many women choose to go back to work, having made great investments in their education and career. These women see great value in continuing to nurture their careers even as they raise a family. And many women may not have the option to stay at home. If you are a single parent, you have little choice but to return to work and ensure economic protection and security for you and your family.

If you plan to return to work as a mother, you will need to give serious consideration to which type of dependable childcare will work for your family. There are many options for childcare today depending on one's income and situation.

One option is to choose a reputable childcare center. The benefits here are many, including a regulated center that has standards of upkeep, caregivers who will always be available, and a safe and clean environment. There is usually age-appropriate care, including potty-training help and a curriculum for learning as your child grows older. Your child will also have the benefit of interacting with other kids as opposed to being at home alone.

There can be downsides to daycare centers, though, such as exposure to germs and frequent infections (although some argue that this strengthens the child's immune system in the long run). Some centers can also be quite regimented, not allowing the free play that some kids need. So, it's important to thoroughly evaluate the childcare centers you are considering for your child. Not all are created equal.

There is huge variation in style of operation, from the regimented schedule of KinderCare to the freestyle learning and care approach of a Montessori school. Reviews from other parents are a great way to learn the inner workings of the center, the behavior of the staff, and the experience other children have had there. There are many online review forums as well. Websites like Yelp and GreatSchools give honest feedback from other parents that can help guide your choices.

Dropping by the center for an unannounced visit is also one of the best ways to see the center in action. It is essential to have questions prepared to ask the center director and other workers. Ask about the teacher-to-student ratio, how often the teachers change shifts, and what the center's approach is to dealing with spirited children or children with special needs. As a parent, you should also pay attention to the dynamic between the center director and the staff. Be sure to talk directly with the teacher/s of the class you are considering, as this person will ultimately be partnering with you to take care of your little one.

If you are a member of a church or faith-based organization, check with them to see if they can recommend childcare centers. They may also know individuals who provide childcare in their homes. This is another good option for many parents. You may desire a more homelike setting for your little one as opposed to the classroom setting of a daycare center. Look around for safety features at the home, such as locks on cabinets and doors, barricades to dangerous areas, and stimulating children's pictures, books, and toys that are important for your child's development.

Ask to see the curriculum that will be used to teach your child. Ask how they approach discipline. Whether you choose a daycare center or home, it's important to do your homework as you find the best home away from home for your precious little one.

Another option is to hire a nanny or babysitter who can come to your home. This option can be satisfying but also terrifying for some, as it entails hiring a complete stranger to help care for your most prized possession in your personal space. On the flip side, it may be helpful for the child to be cared for in a familiar environment. Hiring a nanny, much like choosing a childcare center, requires a lot of research and background work. You are essentially hiring an employee to work in your household. Doing your homework and finding the right individual can help alleviate your fears and give you peace of mind. Some parents install nanny cams that they can access from their cell phones. If this gives you peace of mind, then by all means, do it. However, it is essential to build a sense of trust between you and your childcare assistant.

Several services can help you choose a childcare provider, such as Care.com, Sittercity.com, and eNannySource.com. They offer assistance with background checks and driving records for various caregivers, from date-night babysitters to full-time nannies. Bear in mind that you will need to research how to hire a nanny legally, including taxes for their wages, if you choose this option. Many websites offer assistance and guidance with this information as well.

There is also the option of hiring an au pair nanny. These are usually found through an agency, and they live in your home as they provide childcare. The au pair usually comes from a foreign country and can add some cultural diversity to your home. They may be available at a more affordable rate than hiring a nanny. Again, it's essential to do your research on all individuals you are considering to care for your child and live in your home. Background checks and references are essential. An au pair agency can handle a lot of the background work for you.

Regardless of what you decide, you will need to be comfortable with your choice. It will be essential to pay attention to your child's reaction to your new hire, whether it's a caregiver at a daycare center or home daycare, a nanny, or a babysitter. After a few weeks, your child should show signs of contentment and calm when they go to the facility or when you drop by the center unannounced. You should not be afraid to make changes if you sense that your child is not happy, or that your first pick may not be a good fit for your family. Don't stop searching and evaluating your choice of child-care until you and your child are completely happy and comfortable with your decision.

It is not uncommon for working mothers to feel a sense of guilt for leaving the care of their young child to another. Resist this feeling. Don't think of it as abandoning your child, but rather as getting the assistance you need. Many mothers truly need this help, and many children benefit from not having a tired and frazzled mother or father who can't give their best care and attention. How often do we read stories of parents leaving their child or children unattended in vehicles or at home while they try to get errands done? Childcare help is essential for the safety of your child and for your sanity as a parent. You will find peace and a sense of balance when you get much-needed help in raising your children.

There is an old familiar saying that states, "it takes a village to raise a child". This is indeed true. Childcare is an ongoing, very demanding process. As a mother, you can give your best self to your child, when you make deliberate efforts to surround your child with a caring village of people who can help you raise your children. By so doing, you will avoid many pitfalls, such as post-partum depression, burnout and despair. Your children will eventually grow up and be able to do more for themselves. When the time comes, encourage their independence and personal choices. If you provide the best village for them, they will grow with confidence in you as their parent and in the community that helps to care for them.

Chapter 4:

Work-Life Balance: The Juggling Act

Proverbs 31:13–15
"She seeks wool and flax,
And willingly works with her hands.
She is like the merchant ships,
She brings her food from afar.
She also rises while it is yet night,
And provides food for her household."

M any people realize the importance of striking a balance between work and the rest of one's life. We commonly call it work-life balance. Many strive to achieve it, but this can prove difficult at times. It's no secret that a well-balanced worker will be happier and more productive. Even though many agree with this fact, few know how to make it a reality.

In this chapter, I will share a few strategies that have helped me achieve what I consider to be a healthy balance between my work life and my personal life. I still struggle to maintain this balance from time to time, but with these strategies, my default mode of functioning leads to a sense of balance.

The first strategy is rising early. Proverbs 20:13 says, "Do not love sleep, lest you come to poverty; open your eyes, and you will be satisfied with bread." Of course, a lot will depend on your work schedule. However, this tip can be applied no matter what hours you work. Getting up an hour or two before you need to get in the shower helps you jump-start your day. An early start allows you time for meditation and prayer, exercise, and planning your day. If there are important tasks you hope to accomplish that day, write them down and number and prioritize these items. Rising early gives you time to get organized and ready for your day.

Exercising in the morning is another major plus when rising early. Of course, you can exercise at other times in the day, but I find that early-morning exercise gives me extra energy for the day and helps me stay focused. It boosts my metabolism and helps me maintain a healthy weight and avoid chronic disease. It also helps me handle stress at work. It doesn't matter if I get ten minutes of cardio done or thirty. Any amount of exercise in the morning helps me get a jump-start on my day and has tremendous benefits for my health.

The second strategy is not a new one, but it's important. When you are at work, be fully present with what you are doing. Do not allow personal distractions to affect your productivity. Give 110 percent when at work. In other words, give it your undivided attention and do it well. Be efficient. Be productive. When you leave your workplace, others should remark on how your job was done well.

As a general rule, try not to take work home. This is rule number three. We live in a digital age where technology allows us to transcend the walls of the office and bring work home with us. It's not always possible to complete one's daily work tasks in the hours of the workday, so it seems convenient sometimes to complete unfinished tasks in the late hours of the night or early hours of the morning when you can have some peace and quiet. But this should be the exception, not the rule. If you constantly work late into the night or early in the morning, you are taking time away from sleep and other activities you should be engaging in.

One way to avoid bringing work home is to improve your work efficiency while at work. Often, two workers with similar tasks and responsibilities work at different levels of productivity. One may be able to complete their tasks in the allotted time, while another may not. It is not that one worker is any smarter than the other, but rather, they may differ in time-management skills. This is a question of efficiency.

So, how does one worker become more productive and efficient than another? They may be more organized or better at prioritizing their work, ensuring that more important tasks get done in a timely manner. The more efficient worker may also be more skilled in providing self-care: getting more sleep, exercising regularly, and consuming good nutrition. The more productive worker may not procrastinate as much. She may have a better idea of the difference between work that is important but not urgent versus work that is urgent and needs to be handled immediately. Studies have also shown that little breaks taken throughout the workday can make one more productive. Either way, it is important to work on improving one's level of efficiency without sacrificing the quality of one's work.

A fourth strategy for better work-life balance is to take regular vacations. The need for rest and recuperation cannot be over-stressed. Regular vacations can help restore your energy and outlook on your work. It can help you avoid burnout, and it is a great way to reduce stress. Vacations can be as short as a weekend getaway or can entail travelling to distant places for several days or even weeks. It's important to unplug from work completely when you are on vacation. If possible, don't log on to your work computer or take work-related calls when you are away. Doing so defeats the purpose of your escapade. It's important to learn how to truly disconnect from your work when on vacation so that when you return, you can be truly rested and ready to resume your work duties.

An important question is whose responsibility it is to see that work-life balance is achieved. Is it the responsibility of the boss, the employer, or the employee? After much thought on this matter, I have come to the following conclusion: achieving work-life balance is the responsibility of the individual who seeks it. Whether you are the boss or the employee, work-life balance is your personal responsibility.

In corporate America, it is no secret that happier employees make more productive workers. But at the end of the day, the bottom line for any CEO or business owner is to achieve a profit to keep the business afloat. They may offer their employees tips or assistance with self-care to prevent burnout, but the ultimate responsibility for maintaining a healthy work-life balance rests with the person who desires it.

Perhaps you are self-employed and you are your own boss. Work-life balance is important for you as well. It is even more important for you to maintain a healthy balance between work and the rest of your life. If your health fails, you will not be able to fulfill the necessary duties to keep your company or business afloat.

If you are a stay-at-home mom or dad, this concept of work-life balance still applies to you. If you are working at home, you are still working. You take care of the kids, you may be homeschooling, and you are also performing the duties of wife and homeowner. Therefore, it's even more important to set boundaries on your different roles.

So, what does work-life balance look like? Work-life balance occurs when there is a happy medium between one's source of income and the life that that income is meant to support. The well-balanced person is not only successful at his job or career, but has a good marriage, contributes adequately to the care and well-being of their children, and also cares for their own personal health and well-being. If you give time and energy to work at the expense of your health and personal relationships, you are failing to achieve work-life balance.

We have all seen super successful businessmen or women fail to be good spouses or parents. We have seen the person who is so consumed with work that his or her own personal health suffers. Some lack adequate sleep, find no time to eat healthy meals, or make little or no time for exercise. It goes without saying that in order to achieve work-life balance, one must make time to care for one's health. Without our health, we can do nothing, and we become dependent on others to take care of us. Without good health, it's even more difficult to fulfill our life's purpose. It is for these reasons and many more that work-life balance is essential. But do we actually believe we can achieve balance? The goal of work-life balance may seem unreachable or even impossible to many. But I challenge you to believe that work-life balance can be achieved. Let me share with you a few tips on how we can achieve it.

Tip One

The most important tip may sound like a cliché, but it is true nonetheless: we need to manage our time. Every person has twenty-four hours available to him or her each day. It is how we manage those hours that makes the difference.

The average person does not realize the importance of time. In many ways, time is our most prized possession and our most valuable asset. Our time is more important than even our money and talents. It is the thing that people seek from us before they seek our talent or means. Have you ever noticed that people value your time and presence more than anything else you can give? Think of the last time you were invited to an event or function, such as a wedding or a birthday party. If you cannot attend, it is polite to send a gift. But the person throwing the event usually cares much more about your presence than the gift that you may bring; your time and attendance would have meant much more. The most important tip in achieving balance is learning to manage one's time.

Tip Two

The second tip is an extension of the first: to achieve balance, one must learn to prioritize. We all have much to do at home and at work. The person who manages his or her time well has learned to focus on what's important. What do I mean by this? Let's study a practical example of prioritization.

Picture two working mothers with identical job descriptions and the same number of children. Both have to achieve the same number of tasks each day. They need to get up, get ready for work, get the children ready for school, and transport them to and from school each day. One has found the time to exercise for thirty minutes each day, but the other hasn't. She says she has no time to exercise because of all the things she has to do as a working mom.

The one who is able to exercise may do a few things differently. For example, she may not watch much television. She may ensure she goes to bed by a certain time each night so she can wake up early enough to get thirty minutes of exercise in before the kids get up. The difference in the two mothers is that one has placed a greater priority on the need to exercise than the other and has carved out the time to do it. She has made adjustments in how she manages her time in order to achieve it. She has learnt that eliminating time watching television at night allows her to get to bed earlier and wake up early enough to exercise each morning.

Tip Three

The third tip for achieving balance is making wise choices. We have many options related to work. One can choose to work full-time or part-time, dayshifts or night shifts. These choices go a long way in shaping one's ability to achieve a healthy work-life balance.

Additionally, making wise choices begins well before one becomes a part of the workforce. Most people obtain an education and prepare for the workforce beginning way back in elementary school, middle school, and high school. It's important to make wise choices and to stay focused even as a child in school. Even if we failed to make good choices in education as children, many can still seek additional training and education in their fields of interest as adults.

Many adults make career changes later in life in an effort to achieve a better work-life balance. In order to do this, one has to search inwardly to determine what their purpose in life is. What is that thing that you would love to do even if you were not being paid for it? It is said that if one does work she enjoys, she will never work a day in her life.

From an early age, we need to expose our children to various career options so they can find a good fit for their personalities and temperaments. They can learn about various career choices that allow flexibility in their schedules. They can also learn about professions that make use of technology and allow people to work from home rather than behind the walls of a cubicle from nine to five.

Doing well in school and making wise career choices can set you up to have more control of your work-life balance later in life.

In conclusion, it is indeed possible to achieve work-life balance. However, it takes several important steps to get to that place of personal fulfillment. It starts with making wise education and career choices. It requires skills in time management. It requires one to prioritize and organize their time to use their daily twenty-four hours to the best of their ability.

Chapter 5:

The Art of Saying No

Ecclesiastes 3:1
"To everything there is a season,
A time for every purpose under heaven."

W e are trained from a young age to be people pleasers. A young child is frequently praised for doing things that please Mommy, Daddy, and others in authority, and receives negative feedback when he or she does not do so. It is not a bad thing to use positive reinforcement as a tool to get children to do the things we want them to do. For instance, if little Jenny gets all A's in school, she is likely to be rewarded not only in a tangible way, but in the delights of the happiness of her parents as well. With friends, it's no different. As a child, if you share your toys or treats with your friends, you are more likely to be popular and to receive positive affirmation from your friends.

As adults, this need to please others does not suddenly cease. We continue to seek praise and affirmation from others by doing the things they want us to do. As a result, we often overextend ourselves by taking on more than we should. When asked to work an extra shift, we are likely to respond affirmatively—not so much for the extra pay, but also for the recognition and praise from our superiors. At church, we receive praise when we volunteer for various positions. After all, who doesn't want to give of their time and talents in the service of the Lord?

While there is nothing wrong with volunteering our time, means, and talents and helping others, there are times when we are unable to do the things being asked of us. It's not a question of whether we are capable of performing the task at hand, but whether we have the time and energy needed to perform the task at that particular time of our life. Due to our innate desire to please others, we may take on responsibilities that we are unable to give our best attention to. This desire to please others can thus adversely affect our ability to maintain a healthy balance at certain key times in our lives, such as when we have young children and we are struggling to juggle the many tasks we already have. If we don't know how and when to say no, problems arise. Overextending ourselves then leads to the detriment of our health, our relationships with those whom we love, and our sense of balance.

It can be difficult at times to know when we've done enough and when it's time to pass the baton to someone else. We may feel that we have to keep doing by serving as we have in times past. But when life becomes busy and hectic, it becomes necessary to cut some things out. We may feel a sense of guilt if we do not accept a position even when we know we don't have the time to devote to it. But we ought to realize that others are capable of serving in the roles in question. As much as we may want to believe it, we are not the only ones who can serve in a particular role or perform a particular duty, and it is wise and not selfish to allow someone else to serve, rather than overextend ourselves.

As a busy working mother of young children, you may be talented and gifted, but if the use of your talents takes away from your ability to be a good mother, it may not be the right time to take on that particular responsibility, whether it is overtime on the job or a new position at church. Many mothers of young children do volunteer for various roles, but often it's for activities their kids already participate in, such as a class at church or an activity at school. A mother may find it easier to help with her child's Bible study class or as a teacher's aide at their school. These roles help her stay connected with her children while allowing her to serve in a productive way in the community.

I was once a member of a large church with many young families. It was not unusual for there to be multiple functions, such as birthday parties, baby showers, or wedding showers, all on the same day. As a pastor's wife, I frequently received invitations to attend such functions, and when I was able to, it was a delight for me to attend. But there were times when I didn't have the time to attend or there was a clash in my schedule. Many times, I had to decide whether to attend one event, both, or neither. My desire to please others often caused me to overextend myself at times, leaving me tired, exhausted, and frustrated.

When you cannot attend an event, there are ways to make up for your lack of attendance. Many times, you do not even really need to attend. But if you chose to decline, sending a gift in lieu of your attendance is always an appreciated gesture. The thought is often more appreciated than the gift itself.

It's essential to manage one's time well to achieve and maintain balance. Often, the problem is not a one-time event, but offers to take up ongoing positions. This may happen at one's place of work, at church, or in one's local community. In such situations, it's important to think about the amount of time and energy needed to fulfill the demands of each new role. One of the worst things one can do is accept a position, then be only half-heartedly devoted to it. This helps no one and leads to frustration for you and everyone involved. It's OK to say no when you know you won't have the time or energy to do a job well. Knowing when to say no requires a great deal of personal reflection and deliberation on your part. Remember, it doesn't mean you won't be able to do the task ever, just not at the present time.

Once you determine that you cannot attend an event, it helps to say no in a gracious and timely manner. Do not delay your response in hopes that the offer will disappear. To decline a party invitation, send a simple note to the host saying something like, "Thank you for the invitation; however, I will not be able to attend." You do not need to explain the reason for your lack of attendance. You may have another engagement, and it's OK to state that if you so choose, but you are not obligated to explain why you could not attend. In general, event organizers already know that not everyone who is invited will be able to come. When done correctly, saying no should not adversely affect your relationship with them. You should be able to maintain your relationships, both personal and professional, all the same.

If you have been offered a position at work, church, or in your local community, a more formal response may be warranted. A short letter or note expressing your gratitude for the offer but declining to accept at this time is fitting.

The most important thing is for you to be at peace with your decision. You should not feel guilty for not being able to attend every event or accept a new position or job offer. Rather, you should order your life in such a way that you do not overextend yourself and create unnecessary stress by trying to please everyone.

Chapter 6:

Quality Time with the Kids

Psalm 127:4–5

"Like arrows in the hand of a warrior,

So are the children of one's youth.

Happy is the man who has his quiver

full of them."

Y our kids are growing fast, and before you know it, they will leave the nest and start a life of their own. For the years that they are with you, cherish every moment of the time you spend with them. Enjoy every stage of their development. When they are babies, we mothers give them a lot of attention, but as they grow older, they become more independent and may not spend as much time with their parents. They may prefer to spend more time with their friends or with their electronic devices.

If there were one defining feature of this generation of kids, it's their affinity to electronic devices. You see kids everywhere glued to their tablets and computers. While these technological skills may have some productive role, it's important for parents to limit their use, especially early in life. The American Academy of Pediatrics has recommended no more than two hours of screen time for kids each day. This includes television, the computer, and any other kind of digital device. Too much screen time leads to social isolation, poor communication skills, and poor relationships with others. Thus, it's important for parents to stay connected with their kids as they grow and develop, especially in this age of advanced technology. This will help you develop a better relationship with them, helping you influence and guide them as they make important choices in life.

Recently, I had the opportunity to join my nine-year-old son for his karate class. What a special treat! I thoroughly enjoyed the experience. Not only did I get some much-needed exercise, but my son was able to show me how to do his karate moves, and boy was he good at it. Here was my son teaching me something I did not know. I was happy to share in this one-of-a-kind experience with him. I was happy to see my son maturing and developing talents and interests of his own. I couldn't help thinking back to the years when I held him as a baby, thinking how quickly he had grown into the confident, intelligent nine-year-old he had become.

Spending quality time with your kids does not need to be difficult. The hardest part is having the time, patience, and energy to really be present with them, to really watch them grow and become independent. Whether we are at home with them, volunteering at their school, homeschooling them, worshipping at church, transporting them to their extracurricular activities, or on vacation with them, that time is precious and it goes by fast. Before you know it, they will be teenagers, and they won't need your help in the ways they did when they were younger. Soon, they will be talking about learning to drive, going to college, and meeting that special someone. Stop and take it all in.

At Home

Take joy in the simple things. I enjoy watching my kids eat their dinner, do their homework, play together, and get ready for bed. I even enjoy watching them sleep. These precious moments are irreplaceable, and it's the reason I decided to cut back my work hours recently. At one point, I was working so many hours that I had to hire someone to pick up my kids from school, take them to their extracurricular activities, help them with homework, make dinner, and even get them to bed. This was when I worked the late shift and got home many times after 9 p.m. As they grew older, my kids started to hate those evenings. They didn't like going to bed without seeing Mommy, and they certainly let me know it.

I hated not knowing firsthand how their day had gone. Were there any issues with their behavior at school that day? Many times, I got sketchy information from the nanny, only to have to wait until the next day when I could speak with the teacher face to face to get the full story. When these behavioral issues started escalating, I realized I needed to be more present with my children. They needed me there, picking them up from school, asking them how their day went, addressing any issues of the day, taking them to their extracurricular activities, eating dinner with them, and getting them ready for bed. These may seem like trivial tasks, but to the child, it means the world to be able to interact with their parents and spend quality time with them.

Having dinner together as a family became a special time for all of us to look forward to. At the end of a busy day at work and a hectic day at school, it was refreshing to sit down and have dinner together as a family. It was as if we were saying, "No matter what comes our way, we stand united, and we are here for each other."

It's also beneficial to involve your kids in household chores as they grow older. As soon as they are able, have them make their beds, help with the laundry, and wash their own dishes. I fondly recall my five-year-old daughter demanding to help me load the washing machine or wanting to sweep the floor when she saw me cleaning. Kids enjoy these activities when they are young, and we should encourage their ongoing participation in household chores as they grow older.

At School

For those who homeschool, you get to spend this time with your children as their teacher. You get to decide on their curriculum as well as plan for field trips and other educational activities.

For those of you who send your children off to school, it is important to first decide on the best school for your child. Today, there are various choices, from small, intimate charter schools to private or public schools. You can plan to be there for occasions when parents are encouraged to participate in school activities. Taking the day off for your child's field trip will be a pleasant break from work for you and will make wonderful memories for you and your kids. You might be able to volunteer as a teacher's aide or help with fundraisers. It's important to attend piano recitals, school plays, and sporting events. By doing so, you can watch your child's development of skills in areas you may not have seen before.

So, how do you make time to attend these events? Many parents work long hours and cannot always be at school events. But a little planning and time-management can allow you to attend these pivotal events in your children's lives. You may need to make adjustments in your work schedule. It might be helpful to go in earlier if that is an option to be able to leave work a few hours early. You may be able to switch shifts with a college, or continue your work later in the evening after attending your child's event. Maybe you can opt out of a meeting or reschedule it to allow you to attend your child's event. These are all adjustments that can be made to ensure you don't miss out on important events in your child's life and development.

It's important to communicate with your child's teacher on a regular basis. Attending the biannual parent-teacher conference is a must. But you should also talk with your child's teacher on a regular basis regarding any questions or concerns you may have regarding homework assignments, classroom curriculum, or behavior issues. Remember that your children are spending a significant amount of time at school, and they may be dealing with unique challenges that require guidance and counsel. By closely communicating with your child's teacher and with your child, you can closely monitor any issues they may be facing, such as bullying, peer pressure, or difficulty mastering certain classes or assignments. Engaged parents can intervene when necessary and help their child deal with such issues as they arise with the assistance of their teacher or school principal.

On Vacation

Family vacations should be some of the best times for parents and their kids. Time away from the routine is special and essential for maintaining family unity and togetherness. When you pack up the suitcases and drive or fly off to a pleasant destination, you make priceless memories with your kids that will last a lifetime.

It's important to plan vacations with a deliberate attempt to engage your kids in fun and enjoyable experiences. It could be a long trip to another state or a cruise, or a short day trip to a local theme park, zoo, aquarium, museum, or botanical garden. These experiences enrich the lives of our children and make them more aware of the world and what's around them. I know some children who have never left their local neighborhood, never venturing beyond their local city or community. This is a great misfortune, and it has a direct effect on their IQ and worldview.

Make it a point to discover the world with your kids. If money is a barrier, there are affordable ways to travel and see new places. Take a bus or train instead of a plane. This can be even more fun, and it allows you to see more sites as you travel. Road trips are also a great way to see the sites as you travel to various destinations.

At Worship

It's important to worship together as a family and to teach your kids the value of worship. There is a common saying that the family that prays together stays together. When you depend on a higher power rather than your own strength, you relieve the pressure to do it all yourself. Dependence on God teaches you to surrender your fears and trials, and it gives you a peace that helps you transcend the many trials and difficulties in life. Therefore, it's important to spend time worshipping with your kids, both at home and at church. This helps them develop a faith of their own and a relationship with God that will serve them for life.

Spending time with our children is important; they grow up fast. And it's important for us to be there when they need us to show them how to manage life's trials. That way, when they grow to adulthood, they will be equipped with the skills to face life's challenges. As it says in Proverbs 22:6, "Train up a child in the way he should go, and when he is old he will not depart from it."

Screen Time and Social Media

As previously stated, our kids' screen time should be limited to no more than two hours per day. This includes time spent on their computers, playing video games, watching television, and using any other digital device. Our kids are exposed to electronic gadgets at a much earlier age than any previous generation. As our kids get older, they may start spending time on social media. As parents, we need to decide when they are old enough to have social media accounts, as there are many risks inherent in kids being on social media. They can be preyed upon by predators who may seek to do them harm. They can be bullied or made fun of on social media, and at times they may engage in inappropriate conversation that can affect their reputation as they get older. There are many social media platforms, and our kids will know about them long before we do, so it helps to keep an eye on your kids internet activities at all times. Better yet, maintain open and honest dialogue with your kids, and allow them to come to you anytime they have questions or challenges with something, online or offline.

Essentially, spending quality time with our kids is the best gift we can give them. The time spent with them is priceless, and it will help us stay in touch with them as they grow into teenagers and adults. We will be aware of their triumphs and failures. We will know when they have particular struggles because they won't be afraid to share them with us. We will be able to share words of wisdom with them as they grow older and start making their own choices.

By spending quality time with our children, we will train them to be their best and to aspire toward balance in their own lives so that they can fulfill their life's purpose. They will value us not simply as parents, but as mentors and trusted counselors when the need arises. The time spent with our children can never be replaced, and we ought to make every effort to be there for them.

Chapter 7:

Making Time for You

3 John 2
"Beloved, I pray that you may prosper in all things and be in health, just as your soul prospers."

T his is the self-centered chapter; it's the chapter that focuses on care of the self. As women, wives, and mothers, we are accustomed to nurturing and caring for others, many times to the detriment of our own health and well-being. As Christians, we may be even more self-sacrificing as we serve the needs of our fellow human beings. This is admirable indeed, but this chapter focuses on the need to love and care for yourself, for in doing so, you will be better able to care for others.

In my work as a physician, I have met many people—especially women—who serve as caregivers for others, yet neglect to take proper care of themselves. They take no time to eat healthy, exercise consistently, sleep adequately, or have fun. They give so much of themselves to others that they have nothing left to give to themselves. Some suffer with physical and mental ailments.

I will get right to the point here: If you do not take care of yourself, you will not be able to take care of others. In Luke 10:27, we are given the greatest commandment: to love the Lord with all our heart, and also to love our neighbor as we love ourselves. It is implied in these commands that we already love ourselves. Self-love in this context is not selfish, self-indulgent behavior that disregards others, but an appreciation and care for the person God created you to be. It means you nourish yourself and take care of your own needs in order to fulfill your life's purpose. When you pour into yourself, you are better able to care for others, including your family, your coworkers, and those in need in your community.

Neglecting self-care inevitably leads to physical, mental, and spiritual burnout.

Burnout is a state of exhaustion that many of us suffer from in our busy, overworked society. Many of us do not get enough sleep because we are always on the go, running to and fro. We are doing the right things, such as taking care of the home, the kids, the family, and the church, but too often we neglect to take care of ourselves, leaving us empty with nothing more to give.

If you work hard, you need to play hard too. Playing hard means indulging in fun and relaxing activities like massages, spa treatments, and vacations. Picture sandy white beaches, floral botanical gardens, or musical shows on Broadway. Treat yourself to uplifting experiences and engage in activities that make you throw your cares to the wind, unwind, let your hair down, and laugh a lot. After all, laughter is great medicine.

Let's talk about exercise. Doctors recommend at least 150 minutes of cardiovascular exercise each week. For example, you can work out for thirty minutes five days per week, or for fifty minutes three days per week. This is the minimum amount of exercise we should engage in each week. The benefits are tremendous. Not only will you burn calories and help maintain a healthy weight, you will also feel more energetic, your sleep quality will improve, and you will think more clearly. Many would say that the biggest barrier to exercise is the lack of time. I would suggest that the biggest barrier to exercise is the failure to make it a priority. If we are truly honest with ourselves, we can find 15 to 30 minutes each day to exercise. We may need to cut some things out, or make adjustments in our schedules. But ultimately, if we make exercise a priority in our lives, we will find the time to do it.

What about our diets? Self-care also includes nourishing our bodies so that we can function at our greatest level. Most of us have a basic idea of what healthy eating means.

We need to eat regular servings of fruit, vegetables, beans, nuts, and legumes. The more plant-based our food is, the healthier we will be. But we frequently lack the time to plan and prepare healthy meals. We may eat on the go rather than prepare meals ahead of time. But with a little planning and preparation, it is possible to select healthier food options and eat more nutritious foods.

Another aspect of self-care is getting adequate sleep. The average person today does not get nearly the amount of sleep their body needs. In general, most adults need about seven to nine hours of sleep each day to be able to function at their best. Lack of sleep is evident in people who complain of chronic fatigue and use caffeine as a means to function during the day. This is not ideal. With the right amount of sleep and exercise, one should have enough energy to function without depending on a stimulant.

Self-care also means taking time to indulge in fun activities one enjoys. As I said earlier, at one point in life, I could not tell the last time I'd read a novel from cover to cover. This only happened when I made a major change in my career and reduced my work hours to allow time for personally uplifting activities. It's important to be able to unwind and abandon your cares by indulging in something fun and exciting. This escape from the routines of work and even home life can be rejuvenating and rewarding.

So, how do you find time for you when you're wearing so many hats? You're a wife, mother, career woman, sister, friend, church member, and more. How do you pull away from all the demands on your time to make time just for you? Well, it takes deliberate planning on your part to make it happen. You have to pencil in your alone time on a daily, weekly, and even monthly basis. Each day, wake up a little earlier than your kids. Prayer, meditation, planning your day, exercise, and even meal preparation can all be done in the wee hours of the morning before your house begins to stir. By the time everyone else is up, you'll be ahead of the game.

At work, you may have time for lunch. This is your time. Disconnect for even a few minutes from work, perhaps by taking a walk around your workplace or making a quick trip to the mall. These moments of escape can actually make you more productive and efficient once you get back to work.

It's also smart to get your kids to bed early enough to give you two to three hours to yourself in the evening. You may want to spend some quality time with your spouse or just enjoy a warm bubble bath before bed. Perhaps you want to just sit and read a book. After the kids are in bed, you can do these things and more. It may help to keep your television off. You would be surprised how much time you spend viewing television programs. An easy way to gain more time is to turn the television off. The news media typically runs the same story repetitively throughout the day. You can literally listen to a half hour of news each day and be up-to-date on what's happening in the community and in the world. A good rule of thumb is to turn the news off once you've heard the same story a second time.

Another area where many of us waste precious time is on social media. It's the new rave to be constantly connected to Facebook, Twitter, Instagram, and the like. It can even be addicting for some. Think about it: when was the last time you went an entire day without checking social media? As with the television, you can spend some time on social media, but at some point you need to disconnect from it and live your life.

I cannot end this chapter without saying something about housekeeping. Most working women would admit that it's very hard to find the time and energy for housekeeping. The list of chores and errands involved in running a home is endless. From grocery shopping, to cooking, dishwashing, laundry, dusting, sweeping and mopping. There is no end to the work involved in keeping a house clean. In order the preserve your strength and sanity, it may be wise to higher a housekeeper. This person can come to your home to clean weekly, biweekly or as often as you can afford. If you need someone to help with groceries, gardening, or other odd jobs around the house, there's an app for that. There seems to be an app for just about everything these days. Seek and you will find. The use of modern technology can make your day easier and give you more time for yourself and your family. Many busy women would admit that this kind of help is both rewarding and priceless. It will save time and energy for you to spend with those who matter most, while enjoying a clean and well-kept home.

How you spend your personal time is completely up to you. This is your time to attend to your needs. It may be thirty minutes of exercise, planning a healthy menu for your day or week, getting on the phone to call friends and loved ones, or organizing your schedule. You may want to spend some time in medication, reflection, or prayer. Or you may choose to do absolutely nothing. It's all up to you.

The point is that it's important to nourish your mind, body, and soul before you seek to care for others. This will help you avoid burnout and stress, and it will help you serve others even better.

Chapter 8:

The Spiritual Element

Exodus 20:8–10

*"Remember the Sabbath day, to keep it
holy. Six days you shall labor and do
all your work, but the seventh day is the
Sabbath of the L*ord *your God. In it you shall
do no work."*

G od, who created us, in His wisdom, commanded us to take time to rest from work. He gave us six days to do our work, but said on the seventh day to rest, putting your cares aside. Exodus 20:8–11 reads,

> Remember the Sabbath day, to keep it holy. Six days you shall labor and do all your work, but the seventh day is the Sabbath of the LORD your God. In it you shall do no work: you, nor your son, nor your daughter, nor your male servant, nor your female servant, nor your cattle, nor your stranger who is within your gates. For in six days, the LORD made the heavens and the

earth, the sea, and all that is in them, and rested the seventh day. Therefore the LORD blessed the Sabbath day and hallowed it.

This rest is indeed an interesting concept. Much like sleep is essential for daily physical rejuvenation, so the Sabbath rest is essential for our weekly spiritual recharge. If you drive an electric vehicle, you need to plug it into a power source to give it the electricity it needs to run. If you drive a gas-dependent automobile, you need to stop at the gas station whenever the gas is running low. So too, your physical, mental, and spiritual being needs to be plugged in to its power source at regular intervals to give you the fuel needed to accomplish your daily and weekly tasks. This rest is not simply an act of doing nothing; rather, it's taking time to connect with your Creator, fellowship with friends and loved ones, and reflect on the beauty of creation.

Let's talk about connecting with the Creator. He who made us knows what's best for us. He commanded us to rest every week from our labor as acknowledgment that He is our Creator and Lord. This is a demonstration of our reliance on Him for our very being. Something miraculous happens when we tear ourselves away from the arms of work and indulge in the Sabbath rest. It brings peace, calm, and tranquility to our hearts and minds, and revives our spirits like nothing else can. Taking time to study God's Word and commune with Him through prayer and worship lifts us spiritually to a place where we know no matter what we face in life, He will take care of us.

This time of rest from work is a great time to get together with friends and family as well. There is a benefit to spending time with those in our community that cannot be quantified. We are made to be in communion with others, and we do better when we come together. There are many emotional and physical benefits when we interact in positive ways with others. True fellowship with others allows us to see and feel that we are not unique in our experiences; we are not alone. By isolating ourselves, especially when we're facing a problem or crisis, we deprive ourselves of one of the ways to obtain help and healing. Communion with fellow human beings adds strength and encouragement at times when it's most needed. This is why God said we should not forsake assembling ourselves together, but exhort one another (Hebrews 10:25).

It is also beneficial to take time to admire the beauty of creation. We ought to take a moment to smell the roses—literally. Look around at the beautiful towering trees. Observe as they change colors and adapt to seasonal changes. Go up to the mountains and look at the vast landscape around you. If you can, visit a zoo and look at the graceful, glorious animals. Observe how their design and physical makeup equip them for their environment and help them survive. Many times in our work, we fail to see the beauty of creation and the tranquility around us that can add a sense of peace and calmness to our lives. Spending time reflecting on God's creation can renew our spirits and give us inspiration. Wherever we live, we can admire the beauty of nature and learn valuable lessons from it. I cannot help but think of the words of Matthew 6:26, 28–30:

> Look at the birds of the air, for they neither sow nor reap nor gather into barns; yet your heavenly Father feeds them. Are you not of more value than they? . . . Consider the lilies of the field, how they grow: they neither toil nor spin: and yet I say to you

that even Solomon in all his glory
was not arrayed like one of these.

Indeed, when we look at the beauty of nature and consider the thought and wisdom behind creation, we can't help but gain assurance and peace from the knowledge that this world was created by a loving, intelligent, and artistic God.

It is also spiritually uplifting to consider the culminating act of God's creation: the human body. One of the greatest spiritual awakening moments for me was during my human anatomy class in medical school. As I saw the intricacy of the human body and the purpose-filled detail of each bone, muscle, nerve, artery, and vein, each system from the circulatory to the gastrointestinal, the neurologic to the reproductive, the respiratory to the endocrine, I couldn't help but think of the Creator who designed such an awesome structure in which these systems function in harmony and allow us to serve a purpose. It inspired me even more to take care of my body and to help others take care of theirs.

We ought also to protect and safeguard our mental health. A practical way to do this is to limit our exposure to negativity around us. We need to regulate our exposure to the news media that constantly reminds us of evil's presence in the world. Its constant replay of the worst happenings around us is designed to make us fearful, and it will have us living in a state of terror and anxiety. When we turn it off, even for twenty-four hours, we can focus instead on the victory from sin that was already won by our Savior. We can obtain peace and assurance by focusing on Him.

The spiritual element of achieving balance will also teach us how to look outside of ourselves to understand our purpose. We ought to spend time serving those who are less fortunate than ourselves. If you have the opportunity, join a mission group and travel to nearby neighborhoods or even oversees to help those who are in need. By serving others, we are reminded of how much we are blessed and that we have a lot to be thankful for. We also learn that we do not need material things to truly be happy. I once visited a place where there was great need for medical care. As I served these people as a medical missionary, I realized how content they were with what little they had. As we traveled to one of our makeshift clinic sites, I recall young children singing a cappella at the top of their voices in praise to God. They were not rich and they did not possess great material things, yet they had joy in their hearts that one could feel and hear in their singing.

I had a similar experience when I visited Peru many years ago with my husband. As we ate at one of the school cafeterias, we could hear students singing as they worked in the kitchen. We later learned that they were working to help pay for their college tuition as they worked their way through the school. How happy they were even as they worked to help fund their educational pursuits. By serving the underserved, we learn that there is happiness in service, and that true happiness does not lie in the acquisition of great wealth and material possessions.

Yet one does not need to go far to be of service. Wherever you live, there is someone in need. We ought to seek them out and see how we can be of service to the less fortunate among us. People sleep under overpasses in the great cities of the United States. Many lack food and clothing, while many of us have closets full of clothing we do not wear. Students need help with tuition, meals, and books to make it through college. Families are evicted from their homes every day, not knowing where their next meal is coming from or how they will clothe and feed their children. Even in our own neighborhoods, we can find ways to be of service or to lend a hand to someone.

I once lived in a neighborhood that had a scenic lookout not far from our house. People from all over the city would come to that lookout. They ate and drank as they enjoyed the sights of the beautiful landscape and the scenic beauty of the moon, stars, and planets at night. At the end of each night, paper wrappers, bottles, cans, and cigarette butts were everywhere. My husband and I noticed that one of our neighbors went for a jog every morning. She ran all the way up to that scenic lookout with gloves and a plastic bag in hand, and carefully picked up every bottle, can, and wrapper from the ground. We couldn't help but reflect on how such a simple act could be so powerful. It reminded us that acts of service can be performed in the streets where we live, and that we do not have to go far to find opportunities for service.

The spiritual element of achieving balance is that which takes us outside of ourselves and helps us see the bigger picture. It helps us understand our purpose in life and the part we were designed to play in our community. When we realize the greatness of God and the little part He allows us to play in the lives of others, we are less likely to be bothered by the petty things that go on around us. Instead, we delight in being a part of God's wonderful plan for our lives.

Chapter 9:

Yes, You Can Have It All

Jeremiah 29:11

"For I know the thoughts that I think toward you, says the Lord, thoughts of peace and not of evil, to give you a future and a hope."

---─────────────── ❋ ───────────────---

S o, can you really get to a place of balance where every area of your life is in harmony and working smoothly? Is it possible to achieve this state of being and maintain it? Is achieving balance only a fantasy, something that can never truly be attained?

Some will tell you that you can't have this type of balance; that it's an unreachable dream, and that no one can achieve it. They will say that something in your life will always be falling apart and that you can't have the perfect career, marriage, and family life all at the same time. These remarks are often a reflection of their failure to achieve balance in their own life. I encourage you not to listen to such negative commentary. Rather, chose to believe that you can achieve harmony and success in every area of your life if that is your desire. You will need to surround your-self with positive people who believe that "all things work together for good to those who love God" (Romans 8:28).

If you want to achieve balance in your life, follow the steps mentioned in this book. Keep in mind that not everything will apply to you, but it is my hope that by sharing what has worked for me, others can be encouraged. As a working mother, you will need to manage your time well, prioritize what's important to you, and take deliberate steps to make things work. There are times when things will fall apart and not everything will go according to your plan. When this happens, don't be discouraged; keep reaching for that state of balance.

Remember the hurdling race analogy. Achieving balance does not mean that you will not fall, but it means that you will have what it takes to get up again and keep going. By spending time with your Creator and family, and by taking care for yourself, you can be your best and most productive self. You can lead a successful career and still have enough energy leftover to engage in meaningful relationships with your friends and family. You are here for a purpose, and by maintaining a healthy balance in life, you can achieve that purpose successfully.

Balance requires time management, and proper time management involves getting important things done in a timely manner. One of the enemies of proper time management is procrastination. When a task is presented to us, we may have the tendency to put it off for later, especially if we are in the middle of doing something else. We also may procrastinate if we are indecisive about what needs to be done. I have found that avoiding procrastination not only helps one to manage time better, but also helps prevent and alleviate stress. If you do the task at hand immediately or as soon as possible, it does not become a part of the growing list of things you need to get done.

Another helpful tip for achieving balance is to decide what you want your life to look like and pursue that vision. In other words, envision how you want your life to be, and then embark on a mission to make that vision a reality. This is a daring strategy. It means you have to be willing to make changes if necessary. You have to be willing to take risks. You may need to stop doing some things, while you may need to start doing others.

As a practical example, I was once helping with my son's kindergarten class at church. He was six years old at the time. Soon after, we adopted our daughter, who was then two years old. Almost overnight, I had to make some serious adjustments. I penned a letter to the lead kindergarten teacher explaining that I would no longer be able to assist with the class, as I would have to accompany my daughter to her class. My son was now old enough to attend his class without me. Of course, the letter was met with complete understanding of the situation and well wishes for my growing family. A new assistant teacher was found for the kindergarten class, and I was able to move on with my new duties of being an adoptive mother of a two-year-old.

This is an example of making an adjustment based on a significant change in one's life. We face these types of changes and challenges at various stages of our lives. Change is inevitable, and in order to maintain balance, we have to be able to adapt. Whether we are welcoming a new baby, sending them off to school, launching our adolescent as they leave for college, or making room to care for an aging parent, being able to make healthy adjustments helps us maintain a sense of balance.

There are times when you may need to make a change in your career or in some other significant area of your life. When doing so, you may feel that you owe an explanation to those around you. While it is courteous to let others know why you are making the change, understand that you are not obligated to do so. Your reasons for making a change are your personal business and do not require the approval of others. The disapproval of others is often based on their own personal struggles and has nothing to do with you. Therefore, you should not expect everyone to be happy for you or to approve of your decision. Neither should you allow their disapproval to affect your decision.

I remember making a significant change in my career recently. I was doing quite well in my then-role as a physician and administrator. By all appearances, I was climbing the corporate ladder quite successfully. So when I decided to make a change and leave that position, many were shocked and sought an explanation. I was met with mixed reactions from my coworkers. Some were happy for me and wished they had the gall to do exactly what I was doing. Others were skeptical and lamented my leaving bluntly. When I gave the reason of wanting to be closer to family, one person remarked that one could only have so much of family, meaning she did not see the need for me to make such a change for such a reason.

In cases like this, you need to have thick skin and realize that not everyone will approve of your decisions. But more importantly, you need to realize that you do not need the approval of others. You should press forward and do what is necessary to improve your quality of life and your sense of balance.

In my vision for my life, I pictured being able to get off work at a time that allowed me to pick up my kids from school. As such, I sought a position that would allow me to do that. I envisioned being able to have my weekends off so I could focus on my family and have more time for things besides work. I envisioned having the time to read a good book or even write one, and that is exactly what I did.

Don't get me wrong. Making that change was not easy, but it was worth it.

I was able to achieve a sense of balance that improved my quality of life beyond what money could buy. It improved my productivity at work. At the same time, the quality of my marriage also improved. I had more time and energy for my children and my husband. I even had more time to take care of my own health and well-being.

So, what is your vision for your life? How do you wish it could be better? What changes can you make to enrich your life and make it more enjoyable? Are you stuck in a job that you do not enjoy? Do you get nightmares every Sunday evening as you anticipate the following Monday morning? Do you dread going to work each day? And are you doing it only for the money? If so, you may need to make some changes.

What would you love to do each day even if you were not being paid to do it? What are you passionate about? Maybe you like your job, but you struggle with the hours or the commute. Is there a way to adjust these things? Maybe it is time to start looking at different options and working towards making your dream a reality.

While I certainly encourage making changes in one's life to achieve a better quality of life, make those decisions wisely. Deep reflection and constant prayer should always precede major changes in one's life. We ought to seek counsel from God, who knows what's best, and from those whom we trust and love who have our best interest at heart. Once you make a decision, take the necessary steps to make your dream a reality. Do so with confidence and do not look back. When God is leading, you can't go wrong.

Some may ask how to know when God is leading. This has to do with understanding your relationship with God. If you don't know God and don't commune with Him in prayer or read His Word, you cannot know His voice. If I were to ask you, "How did you know when your earthly father was speaking to you?", you would tell me, "It's because I know my father's voice." It's the same with God. When you have a relationship with Him, you will recognize His voice and His leading.

There will be times in our lives when things will seem like they are falling apart. It's at these times that we ought to recognize that we cannot achieve balance through our own strength. We will need the help of our Creator to ride through the turbulent moments in life. Yes, we will face trials and pain. But as we journey through life, we ought to take the hand of our Creator and allow Him to guide use through it all. It's only by so doing that we can have a successful career, marriage, and family life. It's only by so doing that we can truly achieve balance.

Chapter 10:

Maintaining Balance

Psalm 37:23–24

"The steps of a good man are ordered

*by the L*ORD*,*

And He delights in his way.

Though he fall, he shall not be utterly

cast down;

*For the L*ORD *upholds him with His hand."*

Once you get to the place where you feel you are living a balanced life, it's important to maintain that state of being. Yet achieving and maintaining balance is difficult to do in our own strength. With God's help and guidance on a daily basis, we would make better choices for our lives and maintain a state of calmness and peace. In His Word, God says, "Be anxious for nothing, but in everything by prayer and supplication, with thanksgiving, let your requests be made known to God; and the peace of God, which surpasses all understanding, will guard your hearts and minds through Christ Jesus" (Philippians 4:6–7). When we communicate our cares and concerns to God, He directs our lives in such a way that leads to peace and calmness.

Maintaining balance in your life requires constant assessment of your choices, activities, and priorities. Every day, you will have to decide what is important and seek to accomplish what needs to be done. To maintain your sense of balance, here are a few closing tips.

1. Spend time with God.

He is our Creator, and time spent with Him will reenergize and rejuvenate us. He will give us wisdom to make sensible decisions and choices. He will direct out lives so we can order our steps according to His will. When life gets busy and things spiral out of control, He will help us see how to change course and reclaim our sense of balance. Our reliance on our Creator will take much of the pressure off of us because we will not feel like we have to do these things on our own. He can give us the strength and wisdom to make wise decisions. I am reminded of the words of

Psalm 46:10, which says, "Be still, and know that I am God." These words remind me that I can let go and let God, and that He will take care of me.

2. Be organized.

Use your calendar to pencil in important events and activities. Try not to clutter your calendar, and do not overextend yourself. If you already have a significant event on a particular day, it may not be wise to try to fit another event in. It is helpful to use a daily, weekly, or monthly calendar to clearly itemize your schedule. Each week, look ahead on your calendar and decide what you need to focus on. Each day, look at your calendar to remind yourself of the important tasks of the day. By doing so, you will not forget important events or meetings. You will always be prepared, and preparation will help you be successful at your tasks, whether they involve your work, activities with your kids, or time with your spouse. Being organized will help you focus your energy on what really matters.

3. Know when to say no and say it gracefully.

You cannot be in several places at once, and you should not try to be. Realize that you are only one person. There are times when you will feel like you are being pulled in various directions at once. This is when you need to prioritize. Decide what is most important and what can be disregarded or put off for a later time. Do not feel guilty about saying no. There are times when it is better to say no than to be halfheartedly committed to a project. If you can't give something 100 percent of your attention, you may need to leave it to others who can.

4. Make quality time for your spouse.

If you want a healthy marriage, you have to nurture it. Imagine a plant in your garden. If you water it and make sure it has the sunlight and nourishment it needs, it will grow and blossom into a beautiful tree. If you neglect it, it will die. So it is with marriage and any other significant relationship. You have to give it the attention and care it needs in order for it to become something beautiful. Be deliberate about making memories. Go on dates and keep the romance alive. Take vacations together and leave the kids at home with the grandparents or a trusted sitter. You and your spouse will be much happier if you take the time to nurture your relationship.

5. Make time for your children.

Plan activities with them that you can enjoy together. Take them to the playground, the zoo, or an amusement park. The outing doesn't have to be expensive. As many studies have shown, children care less about the price of the things we buy them; they are more interested in our presence with them. Try to be fully engaged with them in the precious moments that you spend with them.

Too often, we give our kids the leftover energy from our long days. We give our all at work outside the home, then come home too exhausted to really listen to our kids and spend quality time with them. Sometimes a five-to-ten-minute catnap can give you the energy you need to engage in meaningful conversation with your kids, help them with homework, or read them a story before going to bed. Ask how their day was and if anything interesting happened, and listen for the answer.

6. Take time to rest.

Have days when you have nothing scheduled, nowhere to go, and nothing to do. Some of my best vacations are spent lying around in my pajamas all day doing whatever comes to mind. In today's world, it is possible to fill every moment of our day with something to do. We must resist this temptation. It is important to protect our free time by not scheduling something into every moment of our day.

7. Expect bumps in the road.

We live in an unpredictable world. Challenges will come our way at unexpected times. But with a good foundation of support in our relationships with our family, friends, and God, we can weather any storm and make it through to see the sun come up again. Storms will shake our world and threaten our sense of balance, but with the techniques described in these chapters, we should be ready and able to handle any challenges that come our way.

I hope you have enjoyed the thoughts shared in this book. My hope is that by sharing my personal struggles to achieve balance, others in similar circumstances will be encouraged and blessed. Too often, we pretend that all is well while we are struggling to make things work. I have found through talking with others that many times what we struggle with is not unique to us. Others are frequently dealing with similar issues. It is my hope that by sharing what has worked for me, other women, mothers, and wives who struggle with balance will be able to use these strategies to make their lives better. By taking these steps, I hope that you will have a more balanced life that is free from unhealthy stress, burnout, and overwhelming burdens. You *can* avoid burnout from your work and enjoy healthier relationships with those whom you love.

This will ensure a happier and healthier life for you and those around you. May God bless you as you aspire to be the best you can be.